JESUS'
PRAYER
RECIPE

The R.E.A.C.H. Prayer Pattern

JESUS' PRAYER RECIPE

The R.E.A.C.H. Prayer Pattern

Norman A. Peart

Durham, NC

Copyright © 2021 Norman A. Peart

Jesus' Prayer Recipe: The R.E.A.C.H. Prayer Pattern
Norman A. Peart
normanpeart.com

Published 2021, by Torchflame Books
an Imprint of Light Messages Publishing
www.lightmessages.com
Durham, NC 27713 USA
SAN: 920-9298

Paperback ISBN: 978-1-61153-445-0
E-book ISBN: 978-1-61153-446-7
Library of Congress Control Number: 2021918049

ALL RIGHTS RESERVED
No part of this publication may be reproduced, stored in a retrieval system, or transmitted in any form or by any means, electronic, mechanical, photocopying, recording, scanning, or otherwise, except as permitted under Section 107 or 108 of the 1976 International Copyright Act, without the prior written permission except in brief quotations embodied in critical articles and reviews.

For
Dr. Jim Seymour, my prayer partner
over the last 20 years.

Thank you for your listening ear,
pastor's heart, and totally
abandoned commitment
to our Savior.

Acknowledgements

Thank you, Lord Jesus, for the incredible privilege you have given us to talk to our Heavenly Father as children. Thank you also for teaching us how to maximize that communication by teaching us how to pray.

Thank you, Grace Bible Fellowship for being a wonderful church family, that has allowed me to communicate what the Lord has laid on my heart and for you to follow in kind.

Thank you, Carolyn Peart for your ever-present love and support.

Thank you, Christopher Butler, for the work you've put in to edit this work. It's much appreciated!

Introduction

Learning how to pray was a lesson taught in my early childhood. Two prayers that were riveted to my mind are the mealtime blessing and the bedtime prayer.

> *God is great, God is good,*
> *let us thank Him for our food.*
> *Amen.*

> *Now I lay me down to sleep;*
> *the Lord I pray my soul to keep.*
> *If I should die before I wake,*
> *the Lord I pray my soul to take.*
> *Amen.*

Other than an occasional cry for help, these prayers were foundation posts in my young life; giving me the perspective that all I needed regarding prayer was covered.

After coming to a saving trust in Jesus, there was another prayer that I learned called "The Lord's Prayer." This is the Christian's most prominent example of prayer. I am certain that you have witnessed the "Lord's Prayer" recited in its entirety or as the prelude to a personal prayer.

This prayer was Jesus' response to the disciples request of Him to teach them how they should pray (Luke 11:1). The Lord's Prayer serves as an instructional guide, a "recipe" to be followed when praying—"pray this way" (Matthew 6:9).

As I have matured in my Christian walk, specifically during pastoral ministry, my esteem, amazement and dependency upon prayer have grown.

No one could ever claim to be an expert in prayer; therefore, I am not tempted to justify my qualifications for writing this book or arguing why you should read it. Nevertheless, the purpose of this book is to present the Lord's Prayer as the ultimate guide for prayer by using the R.E.A.C.H. approach that aligns with how Jesus instructed us to pray.

This approach has incredibly impacted my prayer life and I believe will do the same for yours. We will discuss this approach in detail in the following chapters but for now let us take a closer look at prayer.

Chapter 1

What Is Prayer?

Simply put: prayer is communication with God in which we reveal ourselves to Him and He ministers and reveals His desires to us. We often fail to value God's role in this latter portion of the communication exchange; nevertheless, He desires an engaging interaction just as we would expect of anyone we're communicating with (Jeremiah 33:3, Proverbs 1:23).

Prayer is the soul's cell phone which gives us unlimited access to the Father. Through this open access we can share our most intimate feelings, thoughts, and desires. Though we have this undeniable connection, our communication is most effective when we are: transparent, dependent upon God and maintain a cultivated prayer life. Let us examine these three attributes of effective prayer.

First, prayer is most effective when there is true transparency.

A person who truly understands the privilege of interacting with the all-knowing God can remove all guards and speak honestly without pretense, revealing their true feelings and petitions. We see such vulnerability conveyed by David in Psalms 22:2 when he cries out to God in startling honesty concerning his feelings of abandonment—"My God, my God, why have you forsaken me?" Rather than rebuking David for his transparency, God endorses it as Jesus uses these exact words to express His own sense of abandonment on the cross (Matthew 27:46). So, prayer requires that we approach God honestly and humbly, realizing that He is the expert concerning us. There is no need to withhold anything from the all-knowing God.

Secondly, prayer is most effective when we realize our dependence on God.

Norwegian theologian Ole Hallesby said, "Only he who is helpless can truly pray." Until we fully realize our great need for God we cannot earnestly pray. God allows us to experience life challenges to serve as reminders that the self-dependency system we often invest in is bankrupt. Through life challenges we come to see the significance and importance of keeping prayer as the basis of our hope; even as we hang on to it for dear life. Let me share an account that clearly expresses this reality.

One morning I awoke to an email with news that a couple in our church had just been informed that their daughter was murdered. Prior to going to bed the night before, my wife and I spent hours praying for this couple who learned earlier that their daughter's car was found outside a home that had two dead bodies in it.

That father and mother hit the hard ground of an unwanted reality as the hope they hung to just the evening before, quickly unraveled. I reached out to the father to express my condolences and to let him know that I would continue to pray for peace and strength during this very difficult time. His response stunned me; "Remind me again, why I pray." Words I did not expect to hear from a seasoned saint, but certainly words expected of a loving father who just learned that his daughter had been fatally shot, multiple times at point-blank range. My response to this father struggling to reconcile what he had known of God with his now seemingly, hopeless reality; "We pray to get in God's will and for our own source of strength."

Prayer is above all an act of dependence for as one author stated; "prayer is the language of dependency."[1] The reality is that we will never truly pray until we are so desperate for God's intervention in our lives, and in this world, that we abandon ourselves to prayer.

Thirdly, prayer is most effective when we cultivate our prayer lives by continually cherishing and engaging in prayer.

This is most evident when we keep prayer as priority in our lives and not just during times when we are overwhelmed by challenges or during life's train wrecks. One reason prayer is not always seen in this way is that it is both a privilege and a task. Proper perspective on prayer is lost when we lose the steadiness that comes from keeping these two perspectives in balance. We must pray when we realize how great an opportunity we've been given—privilege, and long for it in those seasons of having tender views of God—gift. But we must also pray because we are commanded to do so even when we are busy or disappointed with God's working in our lives—task.[2]

God cherishes prayer so much that He allows life's difficulties to impact His children as a reminder of our need for prayer, and through prayer our need for Him. This then is a well-cultivated prayer life that has the fortitude to withstand overwhelming life challenges.

Some of the other particulars of prayer that are often highlighted deal with such questions as when we should pray (time), how long we should pray (length), where should we pray (place), and the words we should use in praying (words). For all of these, the Bible reveals great variation and flexibility—time (Psalm 5:3, Mark 1:35); length (Nehemiah 2:1-5); place (Mark 1:35, Matthew 6:6); and words (Matthew 6:7).

So, prayer then is a vital two-way communication we have the privilege to experience. It is experienced best in a transparent dependency, as we continually seek to cultivate its presence in our lives.

Having considered what prayer is, let us now look at a rationale on prayer that can keep us from praying.

What is Prayer?

1. What is the simple definition of prayer given in this chapter?

   _____

   _____

2. The book describes prayer as "the soul's cell phone which gives us unlimited access to the Father." What other analogies, or word pictures, can you think of to make prayer familiar?

   _____

   _____

3. Why are these three attributes key for our prayers to be most effective?

   - Our transparency before God.

     _____

     _____

   - Our dependency upon God.

     _____

     _____

- Our continually cherishing and engaging in prayer:

  _____

  _____

4. Why should challenges in our lives cause us to think of God's desire to talk with us?

   _____

   _____

   _____

5. Additional thoughts and notes:

   _____

   _____

   _____

   _____

   _____

   _____

   _____

Chapter 2

A Key Issue in Prayer

Why pray if outcomes are already predetermined?

This question epitomizes the challenge many Christians face in their commitment to prayer. Believing that we serve a sovereign and omniscient God, many have reservations about praying for an outcome that is "already predetermined." The idea of "predeterminism" is the reason sporting leagues take great measures to ensure that games are perceived as fair; unrigged with unplanned outcomes. They understand that if outcomes appear predetermined, the leagues will never be able to capture the passionate support and intense engagement of their fan base. For this same reason the question "Why pray if outcomes are already predetermined?" removes passionate support and intense engagement.

There are four arguments for praying that counter this fatalistic question. Let us examine them to encourage our commitment to prayer:

1. We are commanded to pray.

Jesus taught that "men must always pray" (Luke 18:1) and also equated a lack of praying with a lack of faith. Jesus noted that a lack of praying would be an indicator that true faith was not present on the earth when He returns (Luke 18:8). Paul also communicates an incredible comprehensive command that Christ's followers are to pray incessantly (1 Thessalonians 5:17).

2. God longs to interact with us.

Jeremiah noted God's longing to interact with His people through His invitation and also commitment to hear and respond—"Call to Me and I will answer you, and I will tell you great and mighty things, which you do not know" (Jeremiah 33:3). When Jesus introduced His teaching on prayer, He made a statement that revealed His expectation that His followers would pray—"when you pray" (Matthew 6:5, 6, 7).

3. Prayer has a role in God's will.

Prayer is built into the plan of God. We see this in the conditional nature of God's challenge to His people that if they act in a certain way, He will respond accordingly (2 Chronicles 7:14). We also note this as Hezekiah is dying, but because he sincerely prays in humility for God to extend His life, God responds by extending his life fifteen years (Isaiah 38:1-6). Because we do not know when God has determined to work in accordance with our prayers, we ought always to pray.

4. Prayer has a role in molding our will into God's will.

The very nature of prayer, often overlooked, is that God uses prayer as a tool to bring about His will in us. Prayer compels us to ask for God to do what only He can do. This is seen in the Lord's Prayer—"Thy kingdom come, thy will be done" or "Bring your sovereign kingdom desires to rule on earth" (Matthew 6:10). We also realize this when God says "No" or "Not now" to us for that is when God's sovereign rule challenges us as it did Jesus in the Garden of Gethsemane (Matthew 26:39-44) and with Paul when he asked God to remove the thorn in his flesh (2 Corinthians 12:7-10). The reality is that none of us are ever fully in charge and must always be ready through prayer to surrender to God's will.

Again, although we can often be challenged to question prayer's effectiveness and then not pray, we must remember the many reasons why it is important for us to pray. Now having addressed this key issue that hinders us from praying let us now look at how Jesus instructed us to pray by examining the R.E.A.C.H. outline based on Matthew 6:9-13.

A Key Issue in Prayer

1. Why is the belief that the outcome of sporting events is predetermined detrimental to the engagement of fans?

   _____

   _____

2. Why is the view that life events are already predetermined detrimental to people praying?

   _____

   _____

3. How does each of these four arguments for praying encourage our commitment to prayer? Select a Bible passage to support each argument?

   - We are commanded to pray.

   _____

   Bible reference: _____

   - God longs to interact with us.

   _____

   Bible reference: _____

- Prayer has a role in God's will.

  _____

  Bible reference: _____

- Prayer has a role in molding our will into God's will.

  _____

  Bible reference: _____

4. If the concept that events are predetermined is not an obstacle to you praying, what are your top three hindrances? Can you think of any Bible passages to help you counter these thoughts?

   Hindrance: _____

   Bible reference: _____

   Hindrance: _____

   Bible reference: _____

   Hindrance: _____

   Bible reference: _____

5. Additional thoughts and notes:

   _____

   _____

Chapter 3
R.E.A.C.H.

While studying to preach on Matthew 6:9-13, I noticed that the way Jesus taught His disciples to pray could be organized into an acrostic memory tool that spells the word REACH: **R**ecognize, **E**ncourage, **A**sk, **C**onfess, and **H**elp. There is no inherent power in this acrostic itself. It is a simple tool crafted to assist Christians in praying. This prayer pattern we find in the Lord's Prayer is a well-rounded prayer pattern taught by Jesus Himself. I say this about the Lord's Prayer because it wonderfully brings together God's will and our needs. God's will, noted in the use of *Father* and *your*, is highlighted in the R.E. portion of the pattern and our needs, noted in the use of *us, our,* and *we*, is highlighted in the latter portion of the pattern (A.C.H.). Clearly this prayer teaches us that we are not seeking to bend God's will to our desires but rather to bend our desires to God's will, hence the order of the prayer pattern which moves from God to us.

The first portion of the prayer focuses on the primacy of God and His will as it moves us into His presence. Hence, the great concerns of God are noted in the phrases—"your name," "your Kingdom," and "your will." Since God is the only one to provide these results, Jesus' followers are encouraged to faithfully walk in step with God.

In the second portion of the prayer, the focus is on God's place in every aspect of our lives as the prayer invites the power of God to impact our needs and necessities. The second portion of the prayer is remarkably interesting as it deals with three essential needs of humanity, and the three spheres of time within which humanity moves:

1. **Bread**—Asking for bread, or food, focuses on that which is necessary for the maintenance of life, and thereby brings the needs of the *present* to the throne of God.
2. **Forgiveness**—Thereby brings the *past* into the presence of God.
3. **Help in temptation**—Thereby commits all the *future* into the hands of God.

Through these brief petitions we are taught to lay the past, present, and future before God's grace.[3]

The Lord's prayer in its entirety clearly and single-mindedly focuses on God being central in this world, in the lives of His followers, in our everyday desires, in our struggles, in reminding us of who controls our lives, and in the ultimate conclusion of the saga of history. For this reason, as Bible scholar William Barclay stated, this is a prayer that "only a disciple can pray; it is a prayer which only one who is committed to Jesus Christ can take upon his lips with any meaning." It is not a child's prayer for it "can only really be prayed when the person who prays it knows what he is saying, and he cannot know that until he has entered into discipleship."[4]

R.E.A.C.H.

1. What Bible account is the R.E.A.C.H. pattern based on, and where is it found?

   _____

   _____

2. This section of Scripture is traditionally known as the "Lord's Prayer," but why is the "Lord's Prayer Pattern" a better descriptive?

   _____

   _____

   _____

3. The R.E.A.C.H. pattern can be divided into two portions. What does each portion highlight, and what important insights do these portions teach us about God, and prayer?

   One: _____

   _____

   Two: _____

   _____

4. What are reasons why this prayer pattern is most suited for someone who is serious about following Jesus?

   _____

   _____

   _____

5. Additional thoughts and notes:

   _____

   _____

   _____

   _____

   _____

Chapter 4

RECOGNIZE

Jesus teaches us in verse 9 that true prayer begins and is centered on God. This is key for what we think of God determines our expectations of Him and how we approach Him. This first word "Recognition" is a pivotal aspect of Jesus' prayer pattern which sets the direction for all that follows. The designation *Our Father who is in heaven* highlights two key characteristics of God that undergird our prayers.

First, God is personally connected and committed to us.

He is a personal God who is so intimately connected to us that Jesus wants us to use His extremely intimate designation "Father" in our communication with God. This designation highlights Jesus' emphasis on relationship and intimacy. It dispels the myth of an unapproachable and uncaring God and replaces it with a picture of a God who longs for our engagement with Him. Therefore, one of the most incredible gifts in Jesus' prayer pattern is His giving us permission to call His Father "Our Father." Because Jesus commands us to enter God's presence on His terms and on the basis of His relationship with the Father, He also encourages us to use His extremely endearing and familiar designation for God in doing so. The inclusion of "our" in referring to the Father, communicates that all of Jesus' disciples stand in God's presence by grace through Christ alone. It also reminds every Christian to pray for our brothers and sisters, and should hinder a lone wolf or self-centered Christianity.

This understanding that our Father is personally connected and committed to us is powerful when linked with another important truth Jesus taught—our Father is inherently good and will not give the children He loves an eel when they ask for a fish (Matthew 7:10; Luke 11:11). Therefore, we must come to God with a sense of expectancy anticipating the best from Him.

This assumption that God is for us, removes the false and self-focused belief that repetition and length of prayer makes our prayers effective (Matthew 6:7-8). In giving us this prayer pattern Jesus teaches us that our prayers can be just as effective when brief as when lengthy. We do not have to manipulate God, we just have to trust and present to Him our needs. This pattern is a short prayer that can be prayed, even leisurely, in less than a minute. Yet, even short, it is a most effective prayer if prayed fully believing that God hears, can overcome anything, and as a loving Father wants to bless His children.

Let me also note that we must acknowledge that there are some who do not have a positive view of their fathers or possibly of fatherhood. Yet it must be noted that Jesus' presentation of God as Father presents God as the ultimate of what a father should be, thereby denouncing our worst father examples, but also surpassing our best father examples. So, we come to God as the ideal loving Father.

Second, this designation reminds us that the God we are praying to is heavenly.

He is far above our limitations and the challenges we encounter in this extremely hard journey called life. In this opening focus we are called to spend time placing God in His rightful position as being greater than all that we are challenged by. Before praying we must remind ourselves of what we are up against in contrast to who is helping us (2 Kings 6:15-17).

- "Lord, you are greater than my cancer ..."
- "Lord, you are greater than my job uncertainties ..."
- "Lord, you are greater than my spouse's insensitivity ..."

This is vitally important for when our problems loom larger than our God, we are without hope! God is greater and must be seen, repositioned as such. A key response to our understanding of God's greatness is to include praise and thanksgiving in this opening section of our prayer. These actions cultivate a God-focused approach to daily life. No wonder Paul stated that an attitude of thanksgiving keeps us alert in our prayers (Colossians 4:2) and he also commands us to develop an attitude, a cultivated habit, of consistently being thankful—"in everything give thanks" (1 Thessalonians 5:18).

The desire we are to have towards this very familiar but transcendent God is for His name to be hallowed. The root of the word "hallowed" is the same as for the words "holy" and "holiness." The word has the meaning to set aside, to give primary honor, to glorify. Jesus highlights the name of God because in the Bible God's name reveals His true identity and is therefore virtually indistinguishable from the person of God. Therefore, the third commandment tells us not to take God's name, God, in vain (Exodus 20:7). The prayer request denotes that God's name will only be properly honored when He brings His Kingdom and accomplishes His will on earth. The prayer request then is calling on God to magnify and glorify Himself in our lives, His Church, and in all of His creation as the creation's greatest need is to know the only true God. The request is not for God to be God, but for God, the only one who can do this, to clearly make Himself known as God. The first petition in the prayer then is to become our chief concern and focus in life—God's revelation and magnification. In summary, recognition is the first step in the prayer pattern because it causes us to focus on the great God we are praying to and gives us expectations as to what He can do in our life circumstances.

Recognize

1. "What we think of God determines our expectations of Him and how we approach Him." Do you agree/disagree with this statement? If you agree, why do you think this is an important starting point to prayer? If not, how would you rewrite the statement to better fit your outlook?

   _____

   _____

   _____

2. Is there a challenge you are presently facing that can complete the statement "Lord, you are greater than..." Please take a moment to write your challenge in this space and then pray it to the Lord.

   _____

   _____

   _____

   _____

3. Why do you think people don't see God as personally committed and connected to us? How does praise and thanksgiving change that perspective? Is there a Bible passage that highlights this point?

_____

_____

_____

_____

4. Why is Jesus' encouragement to call God "Our Father" one of the greatest gifts given to us in this prayer pattern?

_____

_____

_____

_____

5. Additional thoughts and notes:

_____

_____

_____

_____

Chapter 5

ENCOURAGE

One of the most incredible aspects of salvation is that we who are redeemed are now called to participate with God, and to encourage the accomplishment of His redemptive purpose in this world. This is expressed in the phrase in verse 10 "Your kingdom come, Your will be done on earth as it is in heaven."

The Kingdom of God is presented in Scripture as existing throughout all of time in the past, present, and future:

- In the past Abraham, Isaac, Jacob, and all the Old Testament prophets were in the Kingdom (Luke 13:28; Matthew 8:11).
- God's Kingdom continues to exist in the present as part of human history. Jesus told his enemies that God's Kingdom is "in your midst" (Luke 17:21).
- Jesus told us that God's Kingdom will be in the future when He said that we should pray for God's Kingdom to come (Matthew 6:10).

The idea of kingdom denotes a ruler, subjects, and a realm over which the rule occurs. The ruler is our heavenly Father who exists in a heavenly realm where all that He desires is always and completely done by His angels and He has absolutely no opposition. In this world that is in rebellion to God each of His follower's lives are to be His realm of total rule, as it were, behind enemy lines. Thus, creating an earthly community that seeks to perfectly do God's will on earth as it is in heaven thereby overturning the present evil order. Everywhere our shoes tread, His rule should then be on earth as it is in heaven. Everything we touch should then be under His control as it is in heaven.

Our thoughts, actions, decisions, choices allow God's will to be done on earth as it is in heaven. Therefore, requests made in prayer should be for God to have His absolute desire fulfilled in us. Praying this phrase means that we are progressively submitting all that we are and do to the absolute rule of God in anticipation of His Kingdom rule being on earth as it presently and perfectly is in heaven. There is nothing then, that we keep as our own and outside of God's direction and pleasure. As we noted earlier, this is not a prayer to be said lightly as it reminds us that to call for God's Kingdom to come is to claim that we're fully surrendered to God's desire (John 3:30; Matthew 6:33).

Implied in this prayer is also the desire for the final salvation act to occur that brings all of creation under God's will—Jesus' return. This is why we are to pray for the Lord's return (1 Corinthians 16:22; Revelation 22:20) for only then will this prayer be fulfilled. As hard as we try, we are incapable of perfectly fulfilling God's will. All followers of Jesus are therefore encouraged to pray that what began in Jesus' ministry, what we are now participating in and are revealing the reality of, may be experienced in never ending fullness upon Jesus' return.

This second stage in the prayer pattern calibrates our outlook heavenward right from the start of the prayer. From this perspective the requests that follow should be given in line with God's desires and not our own.

Encourage

1. Why does the phrase "thy kingdom come; thy will be done" must occur so early in the prayer?

   _____

   _____

   _____

2. How do you think James 4:3 "You ask and do not receive, because you ask with the wrong motives, so that you may spend what you request on your pleasures" relates to this opening phrase?

   _____

   _____

   _____

3. Why do you think it is so hard to remember to pray for Jesus to return soon? What are ways that you can remind yourself to pray for Jesus' return daily, weekly, monthly?

   _____

   _____

   _____

4. What do you desire the most to see changed in our world by Jesus' return? Why?

   _____

   _____

   _____

5. Additional thoughts and notes:

   _____

   _____

   _____

   _____

   _____

Chapter 6

Ask

Now we come to the most familiar aspect of this prayer pattern, Asking. I venture to say that most Christians do this more than anything else in praying, I know I do. Yet even with this bias in our approach to prayer, Jesus still commands us to make requests in verse 11 "Give us this day our daily bread." There are four key truths we are taught by this point in Jesus' pattern:

First, we are to look to God for our provisions and for this reason He commands us to do so.

The word used for "give" in this request is a command that denotes our strong sense of dependence and need for God to act on our behalf. The approach also denotes a great expectancy that God will indeed respond to our prayers. This is also the thought of Jeremiah 33:3. The first two aspects of the pattern focus on God and His receiving glory, but this third aspect focuses on those praying as His children. As His children it must be noted that we are not told to bargain or beg for God's provision but must only ask for Him to freely give it to us. No wonder James says "Every good and every perfect gift is from above, and comes down from the Father of lights" (James 1:17a). This need is so great that Jesus even highlighted perseverance in bringing our requests to God as a measure of whether faith exists on the earth when He returns (Luke 18:8). We are so committed to taking God at His word that we are to boldly ask God because He has to be true to His promises (Psalm 23:1).

Second, God is focused on our need before our greed, hence the request for bread and not cakes.

Cakes are wonderful to feast on, but only after our primary needs are met (Proverbs 30:8-9). On the other hand, bread was the basic, foundational item of meals during that time period. No wonder Satan tempted Jesus in Matthew 4:3-4 to turn stones into bread for not only did these rocks possibly look like loaves of bread but this was also a very familiar food item a hungry person would salivate for. The request for bread highlights our human needs in that all of the actions necessary to obtain bread is also highlighted—health, employment, a good economy, a properly functioning government, etc. "Thus when we pray for bread we are praying at the same time for money, jobs, government, business, labor, good crops, good weather, roads, justice, and for everything economic, political, and social. The fourth petition is the politico-economic petition. Here Jesus teaches us to pray for the economic order and for everything that goes into the just production, distribution, and purchase of bread and rice."[5]

This foundational provision by God is also seen in the inclusion of the word "daily." Barclay noted that this word did not appear anywhere in Greek literature and was thought to have been created by Matthew until the word was discovered in a papyrus fragment. Interestingly, the fragment was of a woman's shopping list in which she had written herself a note to buy a certain food item for the upcoming day. He goes on to say that it simply means then—"Give us the things that we need for the coming day. Help me get the things that I need for my meals, my family's meals, …" Therefore, the emphasis is to have us focus one day at a time and not to get anxious for the future.[6]

Third, this aspect of the prayer reminds us to be thankful and content.

John Calvin said that the words "this day" and "daily" teach us to ask so that we may learn to be content with what we presently possess, and not to incessantly drive for "more," or to covet more than our needs require. Note also that asking God for today's bread reminds us of our daily dependence on and need of God, and encourages us to be thankful for what God provides to us.

Fourth, our request for bread reminds us to make social justice a part of our prayers and lives.

This prayer should bring about a thought of concern for others who do not have bread, and a desire to make a difference in addressing this inequality. The *our* teaches us to pray for other people's bread and not just our own. It also challenges those in affluent societies, who can come to disdain bread because of all we possess, not to be comfortable in a "look out for self" outlook. Rather, it entails a desire to have God show us what to do— "Something is wrong in world production and distribution. Something is out of joint economically. This petition should stick in the throat when prayed by full Christians; it reminds us of the wretched of the earth."[7]

Ask

1. What are some reasons why asking predominates our time in prayer?

   _____

   _____

   _____

2. What aspect of life is the hardest for you to remember to request assistance from God as you go through your daily life? Why do you think that is the case?

   _____

   _____

   _____

3. Bread or cake? We can often mistake cake for bread, greed for need, so ask the Lord to show you any prayer requests that reveal this confusion.

   _____

   _____

   _____

Jesus' Prayer Recipe

4. Based on the plurality of the request "our daily bread," who are those in need around you that you can pray for their daily bread as well?

   _____

   _____

   _____

5. Additional thoughts and notes:

   _____

   _____

   _____

   _____

   _____

Chapter 7
CONFESS

The fourth step in the pattern is confession as Jesus instructs us to ask forgiveness for our sins/shortcomings in verse 12 "And forgive us our debts, as we also have forgiven our debtors."

This step should not surprise us since we, as sinful creatures, walk in relationship with a perfect, sinless God. Jesus highlights its significance as He includes it as a regular practice for His disciples, but one which He never had to pray for Himself for He was without sin (2 Corinthians 5:21; Hebrews 4:15). In light of our continual battle with sin, confession is the Christians' necessary response to sinning and desire for a vibrantly intimate walk with God. Confession is continual because our need is perpetual (1 John 1:5-10).[8]

The need for forgiveness is presented as a cost unpaid, a debt. This is in line with rabbinic thought which presented sins as demerits, debts that separated us while good deeds were merits that connected us. For a debtor to request that a creditor wipe clean debts is audacious and shameless. Yet this is the way Jesus teaches us to approach God. We are to come to Him in this "shameless" way! Clearly Jesus viewed and taught that the Father was consummate compassion. Therefore, the person who turns to this Father for pardon Jesus promises will receive the complete removal of debt and of the separation this debt creates (cf. 1 John 1:9). This step reveals the great reality of God's grace since the Bible makes it clear that we have no basis for obtaining God's forgiveness on our terms based on merit, or good deeds, but only on the basis of God's unmerited grace towards us in Jesus (Ephesians 2:8-9).

Since this debt is presented as an ongoing reality it is important to note that there is an ongoing need to call on this unending grace in Jesus. In summary, every Christian is always in redemptive debt, a redemption that is totally dependent on God's grace to them through Jesus, that allows an undeserved relationship with a holy God.

In our request we are not only reminded of our need for forgiveness but also our need to forgive. The latter part of this request takes it for granted, even viewing an inability to pass it on as unthinkable, that we are forgiving the debts of others (Colossians 3:13). This is not the basis for our debts being forgiven, but there is clearly an expectation that those who've been forgiven much will forgive much (Luke 7:47). This addition to the prayer is Jesus teaching us His expectation that His followers will seek to reflect the grace and kindness they've received from God.

Followers of Jesus are to have an attitude of forgiveness that guides them to forgive as they have been forgiven. It encourages them to draw from the deep well of forgiveness from which they have tasted, to then be able to forgive all that is done against them. No Christian can therefore say that what was done against them is beyond their ability to forgive (Ephesians 4:32).

A Christian's forgiveness is revealed in their relationship with God and in their relationship/interaction with others. So, our prayers should include our honest confession of our sins against God to God, and by this reminding ourselves in prayer to forgive those who have wronged us. This reminder may result in prayer for forgiveness for our interactions and for strength to do better.

It's important that we note a key aspect of the order in which this prayer is laid out. We are instructed to ask for our needs before we confess. This does not come naturally for me as I can imagine the same for others who were taught to confess (first) to gain access into the presence of God. We must clear our path before we can make petitions in order to allow God to hear our prayers. So as a first born, very responsible, perfectionist-leaning and son of immigrants I have a strong sense of my offenses and my need to confess in order to make things right and to restore relationship. This has been taught in a very popular prayer pattern (A.C.T.S.—Adoration, Confession, Thanksgiving, Supplication) where confessing our sins occurs before we present our requests to God. But this is not Jesus' teaching. The right to come into God's presence in prayer is based on Jesus' sacrifice, not on the basis of our confessions.

Confess

1. What are the benefits of confession in prayer?

   _____

   _____

   _____

2. Why is "redemptive debt" a vital part of a growing Christ-follower's prayer life?

   _____

   _____

   _____

3. Can a Christian truly expect God to answer their prayers if they do not forgive others for their offenses against them? Read and prayerfully consider Matthew 18:21-35 before answering.

   _____

   _____

   _____

4. Why, like the ACTS prayer pattern, do you think we tend to place confession earlier in our prayers?

   _____

   _____

   _____

5. Additional thoughts and notes:

   _____

   _____

   _____

   _____

   _____

Chapter 8

Help

The final step in this prayer pattern is given in this statement in Matthew 6 verse 13 "And do not lead us into temptation, but deliver us from evil."

This step is significant because it determines the focus of the person praying as they transition back into daily activity. These requests emphasize our need to understand that:

1. We are susceptible to failure.
2. We need God's help.

We must realize that we are weak and susceptible to failure when tempted. We need to cry for help, that God will empower us to come through all such experiences of temptation victoriously.

First, the statement of realization expresses our understanding that we are susceptible to failure when confronted with temptation.

A bumper sticker I once saw communicated this as it stated, "Lead me not into temptation, I can find it by myself." Scripture teaches that God never leads us into temptation with an intent of drawing us into doing evil because His holy nature cannot even consider such an option (James 1:13).

We can remove the interpretation that we're asking God to not intentionally lead us to sin. But a distinction can be made that God allows us to be tested, which denotes that we're allowed to go into difficult circumstances to test and encourage our faithfulness. Tempting and testing are similar in that sin can result in both cases, yet they are dissimilar in that temptation has a negative purpose whereas testing has a positive purpose.

The primary meaning in the first part of this verse then is that in the midst of being examined by God we would be kept safe from ourselves and our propensity to sin, or to fail. The prayer request may then be for God to help us to not sin when we are led into testing situations so that our faith will be proven and empowered by the experience.

Second, the statement of realization is for God's help.

This is highlighted in the fact that God can provide protection even in the midst of tests that deeply challenge faith (2 Peter 2:9). We are asking the Lord to keep us from the forces of evil that are seeking the worst for us. There is a specific evil that is noted in the second part of the verse that is more accurately translated "from *the* evil." The definite article can be used in reference to either evil or to the Evil One. This probably refers to Satan whose desire is to defeat the people of God because he cannot defeat God. Since Satan and his emissaries are always at war with those who trust in God our greatest recourse is to have God deliver us. This overall petition may be best paraphrased as—"Do not lead us into a testing of our faith that is beyond our endurance, but when testing does come, deliver us from the Evil One and his purposes."[9]

As it is important at the beginning of this prayer pattern to recognize God as the all-powerful glorious one that He is, it is also vitally important to recognize God in the same light at this point in the prayer. A common error that is made is to see Satan as a counterpart, or rival, to God. Scripture never presents Satan in this way but rather presents him as the one who must even come before God to report and gain permission from God in order to act, especially against God's children (Job's experience in Job 1). If the people of God understand that they are not powerful enough in themselves to defeat Satan and that God is supreme over all, including over Satan, then they will totally depend on God for their victory over Satan. There is no greater evidence of this than to cry out to God continuously for protection, empowerment, and victory in life knowing that this is the only means by which spiritual victory can occur.

Help

1. Why does Jesus end the prayer pattern with a request for help? What benefit is there to the person ending their prayer time to be reminded of their need?

   _____

   _____

   _____

   _____

2. Can you think of prayer accounts in the Bible where a person praying focuses on their need for God's assistance? How did God's provision of assistance make a difference in that person's life and service to the Lord?

   _____

   _____

   _____

   _____

3. What is the similarity and contrast between being tempted, and being tested? Does our response make a difference in determining the outcome?

_____

_____

_____

4. Can you think of any presentations in the media, or social images that present God and Satan as equally matched rivals? How have such communications adversely affected you, or others you know?

_____

_____

_____

5. Additional thoughts and notes:

_____

_____

_____

_____

_____

Chapter 9

REACH Out and Bring Him In!

Our final step is to put what has been presented into practice. One day I was sitting in church listening to a sermon when the young millennial preacher referred to the lyrics of the song "The Message" by Grandmaster Flash and the Furious Five. This song addressed the challenges of life and was recorded years before the speaker's birth. As he said the lead into the chorus—*Don't push me, cause I'm close to the edge*—I was amazed to hear many in the congregation, both young and old finish the chorus—*I'm trying not to lose my head*. It was a reminder that life's challenges are universal, and for this reason, connect us even across generations.

It is this shared experience of life's challenges that allows us to understand the importance of prayer. Because life is challenging, the Bible presents prayer as the act that brings God into our circumstances to provide strength and assistance in our time of need. This is what I used to see in professional wrestling when I was growing up. There were tag team matches that pitted teams of wrestlers against each other. When a wrestler was overwhelmed by his opponent, the only thing on his or her mind was to move their partner from the outside of the ring to the inside to help them. This was initiated by the in-ring partner tapping their partner's hand so that this more powerful person could come in and vanquish the opponent. When the challenges of the fight had overwhelmed them, and they were now at the end of their ability to fight and win, that is when the full focus of the in-ring, in-battle, partner reached out for help that was greater than what they had to offer. This is how the couple felt that I described earlier, whose daughter was murdered. As they continue to be stunned and shaken by their great loss and law enforcement's inability to apprehend their daughter's murderer, I've been blessed to see them bring God into their ongoing battle with life, to gain new strength to battle and excel in life through prayer.

This is one of the key characteristics of prayer, as we realize that our greatest need in life, with its various challenges, is to get God to "tap in" to accomplish what we cannot. In reality, our best battle plan is to have God in the ring more than we are for our greatest strength is when we're in constant dependence and communication with Him. This perspective is so important that Jesus says that continued engagement and commitment to this kind of prayer is an indicator of faith's presence in our world (Luke 18:1-8).

So, are you ready to begin cultivating this kind of prayer relationship as you R.E.A.C.H. to God? I know it will be the most important commitment you will ever make.

REACH Out and Bring Him In!

1. What areas of life do you presently need God to "tap in" to accomplish what we cannot?

   _____

   _____

   _____

2. What aspects of your life presently (work-life balance, busy schedule, over commitment, etc.) keeps you from continually seeking to have God stay engaged and depended on in your daily life?

   _____

   _____

   _____

3. Consider at least 3 "next steps" to make daily prayer a reality and/or priority in your life.

   _____

   _____

   _____

   _____

4. Additional thoughts and notes:

_____

_____

_____

_____

_____

About the Author

Norman A. Peart is the founding pastor of Grace Bible Fellowship in Cary, North Carolina, where he has pastored for twenty-six years. He is a police chaplain with the Cary Police Department. He has served as an adjunct at the University of North Carolina at Chapel Hill and at Southeastern Baptist Theological College and Seminary.

Norman is a sociologist, pastor, and author. He received his Ph.D. from Michigan State University and his Master of Divinity and Master of Theology degrees from Grand Rapids Baptist Seminary. He is the author of *Separate No More: Understanding and Developing Racial Reconciliation in Your Church*.

Norman and his wife, Carolyn, live in Fuquay Varina, North Carolina.

Connect with Norman online:
facebook: norman.peart.1
normanpeart.com

Endnotes

1. Grudem, W. A., Grudem, E., & Grudem, W. A. (2005). In *Christian beliefs: Twenty basics every Christian should know* (p. 48). Zondervan.

2. It is important to realize that there are many things we receive as a gift in our lives that we must continue to put work and effort into that also challenge us to cherish them even when we may not feel driven to do so. For example, Psalm 127 calls children a gift/blessing from the Lord. But if you have children, or are honest about the times you were a challenge in your upbringing, you know that child raising can be a task! Children are both a gift and a task.

3. Barclay, William, (1975). *Gospel of Matthew volume 1*. (p. 199). The Westminster Press.

4. Ibid.

5. Bruner, Frederick Dale, (1987). *The Christbook: A Historical/Theological Commentary: Matthew 1-12*. (p. 250). Word Pub Group.

6. Barclay, William, (1975). *Gospel of Matthew volume 1*. (p. 217). The Westminster Press.

7   Bruner, Frederick Dale, (1987). *The Christbook: A Historical/Theological Commentary: Matthew 1-12*. (p. 250). Word Pub Group.

8   Six Reasons why our prayers are not answered:
    i. Not confident (1 John 5:14).
    ii. Cherish sin in our hearts (Psalm 66:18).
    iii. Man-centered, not God-centered (James 4:3).
    iv. We don't believe God (Matthew 13:58).
    v. God is testing our faith and belief in His command (Luke 18:1).

    - God wills that you keep praying to test your perseverance.

    - George Mueller prayed for 52 years and saw many get saved. He had two people who did not. They trusted in Jesus at Mueller's funeral.

    vi. God is doing something every time you pray and He will show you that every prayer worked at a later time (Matthew 6:7-8).

9   Hagner, Donald A. (1993). *Word Biblical Commentary Volume 33a, Matthew 1-13*. (pp. 151-152). Word Books Publisher.

www.ingramcontent.com/pod-product-compliance
Lightning Source LLC
Chambersburg PA
CBHW071316060426
42444CB00036B/3079